QUININA J. SINCENO

All Scripture quotations, unless otherwise indicated, are taken from the New King James Bible, Copyright © 1982. All rights reserved.

PRAYER101: the secret place
Copyright © QuiNina J. Sinceno 2020

All rights reserved.

GDI Enterprises, LLC.
New Orleans, Louisiana

Printed in the United States of America
First Edition: February 2020

The Library of Congress Cataloging-in-Publication Data
Sinceno, QuiNina
Prayer 101: the secret place
QuiNina J. Sinceno. -1st Ed.

Summary: QuiNina J. Sinceno gives a modern-day interpretation and revelatory teaching of the model of prayer given by Jesus Christ when asked, "Lord teach us to pray" by a disciple who had a desire to learn.

Paperback ISBN-13: 9780578895772
Hardcopy ISBN-13: 9781087958132

Other books by QuiNina J. Sinceno:
SELAH: Poetry that Speaks
Life of JOY: The Key to Transformed Living
www.quininaj.com

CONTENTS

Foreword   9
Introduction   11

PART I | *Posture of Prayer*
State of the Heart   19
Faith Factor   31
The Secret Place   47
Enter His Gates   61

PART II | *As We Pray*
Who Art in Heaven   73
Hallowed be Thy Name   81
Thy Kingdom Come   79
Our Daily Bread   99

PART III | *Hindrances to Prayer*
Let it Go   105
Just Believe   111
No Dead Weight   121

PART IV | *The Kingdom Established*
Sovereignty   129
And it IS SO   131
Teach Me How   133

Afterword   135

This book is dedicated to the next generation of Prayer Generals and Warriors of the Kingdom. I pray you arise as the army you are and declare heaven on earth. May you experience the power of prayer to a greater degree than the generations who have preceded you with miracles, signs, wonders, and manifestations of the glory of God.

Love,
@QuiNinaJ

FOREWORD

From the first time I met QuiNina, I knew she was a conduit with a wealth of knowledge, revelation, and, more importantly, a diligent prayer warrior. She had all the qualities of someone that I knew would be a significant asset to not only our new church plant, but also to the advancement of the Kingdom of God and His people. She has embodied the perseverance and faith to see prayer manifested in individual lives, situations, organizations, and businesses. Today, as I write this foreword to her captivating prayer book, I share words that I always hoped, and in many ways knew I would have the chance to write.

Prayer is something that has always been an intriguing topic for any level of a prayer journey. Whether you have never prayed before or consider yourself an expert in intercession prayer, QuiNina releases wisdom that anyone can utilize and apply at any given moment for any circumstance.

This book provides a valuable window of not just information; PRAYER101 is a treasure chest with many elevational gems that have been cultivated through lifelong practices and experiences. This prayer treasure chest has real-life applications that are not complicated and overly deep to the understanding but is empowering enough to ignite a hunger and passion for advancing your prayer life.

I encourage you today as you open this treasure chest to prepare yourself to elevate your prayer life and receive the wisdom needed to see the reward revealed here on earth. Your tenacity and dedication to develop prayer will help you grow in every area of your life. This book is a must-have treasure for any person wanting more through prayer.

Apostle Lamont Bigham

Gateway Embassy Ministries, *Senior Leader*

New Orleans, LA

INTRODUCTION

Let us pray.

Father, I thank you for the person reading this book. As we prepare to embark upon this journey of discovering the purpose of prayer, reveal unto us the power of prayer, shift us into a continuous prayer posture and transform our hearts for prayer. We believe that prayer is a privilege granted to us to embrace Your presence, speak to You, and hear from Holy Spirit. Open the eyes of our understanding to be enlightened by the illumination of Your word concerning prayer through every word penned that will follow. In Jesus Name Amen

Let's get in-to-it...

Throughout humanity's existence, we have always had a proclivity and innate awareness of a need to connect to unseen deities through prayer. No matter the deity of choice, somehow, we as humans have an instinct that tells us we must have a form of communication to our perception of the divine. Every form of worship has a form of prayer for every deity that each religion believes in as their god. As Christians, believers of the Holy Bible, we believe prayer is our primary connection to our God. According to our declaration of faith, every believer in God is to have what we call a "prayer life," meaning prayer should be an intricate part of our daily living. As a matter of fact, Scripture tells us to pray without ceasing. Unfortunately, somehow as generations went by, we have drifted further and further away from prayer as a lifestyle and state of mind. But I believe a new day is dawning. Not only are we on the verge of a great wave of prayer, but we are also on the cusps of what I am seeing is the greatest harvest of new believers to accept Jesus Christ as Lord and Savior known to humanity with miracles, healings, signs, wonders, and manifestations of glory attached to an uncommon release of wealth. And prayer is going to get us there. Doesn't it sound awesome? Can you see it? Wow, that would be amazing, wouldn't it? It is definitely possible. My prayer is that this book, Prayer 101, strikes your spirit in such a way that it lights the match in you for such a great move of God.

As you read, expect to receive instructions, experience an illumination of Scripture, and a new revelation and fire for prayer through the teachings of Jesus Christ when he took a moment to mentor His disciples on how to pray. What better way to guarantee your prayer than to pray according to the guidance given by the Son of God, the one whom you pray in the name of. I strongly believe that when one does not have an expressed joy in praying it is primarily because they have not seen its success. I doubt anyone would stop praying if their prayers are noticeably answered. It is only logical to think that if prayer is working and producing results in my life, I would dare not walk away from it. To a believer, prayer is our strengthening agent; it is the secret place we go to be encouraged, recharged, commune, and receive instructions from Our Heavenly Father.

Prayer to a Christian is like the phone booth to Clark Kent as he transformed into Superman to fight off all evil that threatened those he loved.

Just in case you are not into superheroes, let me explain, and if you are, just humor me for a moment if you will-with the cliff note version. The main character of Superman, the movie, Clark Kent, whose birth name was Kal-El was born on Krypton to Jor-El and Lara. He ended up with earthly parents after being forced to leave his planet Krypton and later discovered he had special abilities. He was raised by his earthly parents with values and morals and often had to hide his identity. Later he discovered his full strength, but his identity still could not be exposed to the world, so outwardly he would wear unassuming attire so that to the earthly eye, he would appear to be humble, lowly, meek, and even weak. Posing in the disguise of a journalist, he could easily be unnoticed, but when trouble would arise, he would quickly steal away to a secret place (a phone booth, in the older days) and return as a man of unmatched strength.

Prayer does the same for the believer! When we steal away to the place of prayer, that physical place is instantly transformed into our phone booth, our bat cave, our command center. Today that secret place can be your car, office, bathroom at home, a public restroom, or even a mental place and not a physical location. I will explain that later, but the point is tremendous power is made available through the effectual and fervent prayers of the righteous through faith. And it is all available for you to participate in at any time for any reason. There are even those of us who live in a place/state of prayer ready to go before the Father on another's behalf at any given moment.

What is Prayer?

So, what exactly is this praying thing that I am talking about, you may say. Well, prayer, for the believer, is communicating with God. Just as communication is a two-way exchange, so should prayer be. When praying, people tend to turn prayer into a one-sided dialogue where one tells God all about their sorrows and concerns. It is unfair and delusional to believe a conversation has occurred if there was no exchange between two or more subjects. Thus, to think that when praying only telling your side of the story of your life is not only a delusional prayer but also ineffective and an incorrect one at best. Therefore, I believe so many have become so withdrawn from prayer. Because there seemingly have been no answers to their prayers, but the truth very well may just be that they have yet to take the time to receive the answers for their petitions. Prayer is not just an outlet, but it is also an input. Yes, we literally lay-out before God ourselves, our concerns, and the desires of our hearts, but we are also to allow God to input into us the wisdom, revelation, and instructions of His will concerning those very things we have lain out before Him. That is the conversation worth having. You speak to God, and He speaks to you.

STATE OF THE HEART

So, how is your heart these days? Have you accepted Christ into your heart by believing that He is the Son of the True and Living God? If you have not but desire to accept Jesus Christ as your Lord and Savior, I encourage you to take a moment before going further. Simply confess that Jesus is Lord over your life, believe that He is the Son of God who died for your sins and God raised Him from the dead; and you are now saved my friend. Welcome to the body of believers, the family of the Kingdom of God.

That if you confess with your mouth the Lord Jesus and believe in your heart that God has raised Him from the dead, you will be saved. For with the heart one believes unto righteousness, and with the mouth confession is made unto salvation. For the scripture says, "Whoever believes on Him will not be put to shame." Romans 10:9-11

The most important prayer that anyone can ever pray is a prayer of repentance to accept Christ for salvation. The condition of your heart as a follower of Christ qualifies you to pray in the name of Jesus; it is essential to your prayer life.

Believe Me that I am in the Father and the Father in Me, or else believe Me for the sake of the works themselves. "Most assuredly, I say to you, he who believes in Me, the works that I do he will do also; and greater works than these he will do, because I go to My Father. And whatever you ask in My name, that I will do, that the Father may be glorified in the Son. If you ask anything in My name, I will do it. John 14:11-14

Believe that He is.

Why pray in the name of one whom you do not yet believe in? We must first believe in Christ because we pray in His name. I believe, that because you are reading this book, you have accepted Christ into your life and believe that He is the Savior. But the belief that I am speaking of is the belief that God hears you and answers. Taking the time to pray is not a wasteful act or an act where one should be unsure whether God answers and is concerned about your affairs. After all, we are approaching God in the name of Christ, the one who has prayed for us. Knowing and understanding that Christ first prayed for us is grounds for a belief in the prayer's value, which is why we believe when we pray. It is so easy to look at the situations and circumstances of this world that would imply that Jesus is not still sovereign and operative as the savior of the world. But I assure you He is and if you would just take the chance of believing that when you pray, God hears you, and when you expect an answer, you will also see that God's ear is open to the cries of the righteous.

Being the righteous means that we are also heirs, and being heirs, we have a right to speak with our Father. As children of admiration our hearts find delight in spending time hearing from our Father. Therefore, when we approach God, we approach Him knowing that He wants to hear from His child. There is a significant difference between children who fearfully approach their father with a request, verses children who approach their father with confidence in knowing that their father favors them. The posture of dialogue of the two would differ quite substantially. There is no feeling like the feeling of knowing that your Father wants to hear from you and spend time with you. Just as a child who knows that he/she is wanted experiences and embraces the acknowledgement that sonship adds to their heart, it creates a feeling of being the beloved. We have been adopted into the royal family of God; He loves you so that He has given you the right to access His attention.

Therefore, when you approach God, you approach Him as a son in the name of your elder brother Jesus boldly. The reason you approach boldly is because the blood of Jesus purchased your right for adoption. We serve a holy God, and if it were not for Jesus redeeming us from the penalty of sin, we would not be able to approach God because of our sin. It was through Jesus's blood that we received the opportunity for redemption and forgiveness. This means the blood has covered our sin. It literally paid for our sins, so when God sees us, He no longer sees our sin when we approach Him as an heir in the name of Jesus Christ. Instead, He sees the DNA of the blood of His son which now covers us because of our acceptance of Christ.

So, what does this mean? It means our hearts should be centered on the truth that we have not paid the price to approach God for our sins and are not worthy, but because the blood has been atoned for us, we are now worthy. It was not of our works; therefore, we have no right to boast but are to be thankful for The One, Christ, of whose blood gives us access. The blood that was shed through love for us should compel us to have love and compassion for others. We ought to allow prayer to be done out of pure love, which should be shed abroad in our hearts. Prayer is a love tool; it is not meant for control, selfishness, harm, or manipulation. If done through the motives of either of those, your prayer automatically becomes ineffective and has entered into error through prayers of witchcraft.

It is quite asinine to think we can pray to an all-knowing God with a heart that has been tainted by motives that do not exemplify the nature of who He is and receive a favorable response from Him. That my dear, is the epitome of hypocrisy and is what I believe to be one of the reasons many have been so repelled by prayer. I am sure someone you know who has misused prayer may have crossed your mind and you can remember how turned-off you felt. Jesus himself said, "These people honor me with their lips, but their hearts are far from me." Matthew 15:8 The incorrect images of what prayer really is has caused quite a bit of damage, but I am so happy you will change that. However, I admonish you not to be judgmental towards those you know of that have entered a state of error. The truth is they simply have a heart problem. It can be corrected. Therefore, we are making sure yours is in check first and are learning of other things to watch out for so that your prayers will not be hindered.

Identifying heart problems.

Any time you begin to pray for any reason other than a reason for restoration, edification, comfort, and salvation, there could be an indication of a heart problem. All wrong motives are a manifestation of a heart problem and must be addressed if you desire to go to another level in your prayer life or even begin an effective prayer life. There are specific indications of heart problems which cause hindrances to your prayers, but we will get deeper into those hindrances later in another chapter. For now, just remember to make sure your motives are in line with the nature of God. God is love. Just in case there are any discrepancies of what Love really is, here is a little help.

Love endures long and is patient and kind; love never is envious nor boils over with jealousy, is not boastful or vain glorious, does not display itself haughtily. It is not conceited (arrogant and inflated with pride); it is not rude (unmannerly) and does not act unbecomingly. Love (God's love in us) does not insist on its own rights or its own way, for it is not self-seeking; it is not touchy or fretful or resentful; it takes no account of the evil done to it [it pays no attention to a suffered

> *wrong]. It does not rejoice at injustice and unrighteousness but rejoices when right and truth prevail. Love bears up under anything and everything that comes, is ever ready to believe the best of every person, its hopes are fadeless under all circumstances, and it endures everything [without weakening]*
> 1Corinthians 13:4-7

Another indication of a heart problem also shows through fear. We spoke about disbelief, also an indication, earlier. But perfect love of a pure heart casts out all fear. Thus, when we prepare to pray, we do not approach God from a place of fear but from a place of confidence in the love He has for us and the love we have for Him. I have found most people who do not have a healthy relationship with God tend to approach God in a state of lowliness or fear.

They tend to use words like, "if it is your will" or "God can you" as a plea out of a lack of knowledge and experience with who God is. If that has been you, it is ok; you are in good hands now. Then there are those whose arrogance has gotten the best of them, and they speak to God as though He is their subordinate of sorts. You will tend to hear them say things in a nature of command towards God. These individuals have usually had a history with God answering previous prayers and have slowly stepped outside of humility and the fruits of the spirit and have entered more-so into thinking they have the authority to command Holy Spirit, angels, or even God. It may seem farfetched reading it, but it is true and does happen.

On the flipped side of the spectrum, an individual who has a healthy relationship with God will often approach Him in prayer quite differently because out of their relationship, fellowship, and experience with God, they know His Word. Therefore, instead of asking God if it is His will, they are like the child who says, "Daddy you said I could" or "Father I believe your Word that says…and I thank you" out of a place of belief in their hearts of what their Father has already said. Note, it is not out of arrogance or fear but from a place of confident faith as a child believing their father's words. As a child whose heart safely trusts in their father is how we should approach prayer. Your heart reveals how you handle your sonship; it determines your entitlement. So, I ask again, how is your heart these days?

FAITH FACTOR

But without faith it is impossible to please and be satisfactory to Him. For whoever would come near to God must [necessarily] believe that God exists and that He is the rewarder of those who earnestly and diligently seek Him [out]. Hebrews 11:6

What is faith?

Some time ago, there was a popular tv show named Fear Factor. It was a type of game show. The show's objective was to test its participants' resolve by putting them into situations that terrified them. Depending on their fear they would be tested in a particular area. Millions would watch this show just to see what the next mission would be. There were snake pits, spider tanks, extreme heights, closed quarters, cages, and many other terrifying traps. Their fears became the factor; it was the only thing preventing them from winning or escaping. The winner was always the individual who conquered their fear by completing the assigned task in its entirety.

We are talking about faith in this chapter, but that concept is so wildly accurate, and I believe it also parallels with the principle of faith in prayer. Our faith is one of the main factors in prayer. Strengthening one's faith gives prayer a conquering persona. What do I mean? When you believe that no matter what pit you are in or what seemingly deadly circumstances are around you, God will answer because He hears you, it makes your prayers powerful. Your faith is like voltage, the more potent your faith, the greater the voltage. We all know how powerful high voltage electricity is. Your faith can be like lightening that strikes voltage into your prayers, giving it a charge that does damage to any and everything that has tried to be a hinderance to you. It is your factor!

Faith is your influence that contributes to your results in prayer. How significant is your influence? It can only be determined by you and your choice of the measure by which you believe. There is a scripture that I am reminded of that is used quite often that I believe it is yet to be fully unpacked by revelation. Shall we take a look?

> *So, Jesus said to them, Because of your unbelief; for assuredly, I say to you, if you have faith as a mustard seed, you will say to this mountain, 'Move from here to there,' and it will move; and nothing will be impossible for you.* Matthew 17:20

Many times, this verse has been used as a justification for small amounts of faith. I do not believe that was what Jesus was saying to us. He was not giving us a pass for having only a little faith. As a matter of fact, throughout His ministry, He was often grieved by the lack of faith that people had, even his disciples at times. Instead, just as Jesus usually spoke in parables to bring clarity, He used an analogy in this exact instance with the mustard seed. Yes, mustard seeds are, in fact, one if it not the smallest seeds among trees but grows into an enormous bush among herbs which develops into a large tree of herbs. This tells us that our faith begins as a seed but has the potential to grow beyond limits. Jesus said when faith is as a mustard seed, you will speak to the mountain. "Will" is a word in a futuristic tense meaning "to come", therefore, when your seed grows you will speak and when you speak your mountain will move. Thus, nothing shall be impossible for you because your faith, which was once a seed, has willingly allowed itself to grow into a faith tree. Here is a little proof of this same analogy of the mustard seed that Jesus also spoke of when teaching about the Kingdom of God.

> *Then He said, "To what shall we liken the kingdom of God? Or with what parable shall we picture it? It is like a mustard seed which, when it is sown on the ground, is smaller than all the seeds on the earth; but when it is sown, it grows up and becomes greater than all herbs, and shoots out large branches, so that the birds of the air may nest under its shade."* Mark 4:30-32

I believe Jesus intends for your faith not to stay as a seed but grow and grow massively. Others need your faith to grow, just as birds need trees for shade. Once you have gotten to a place where you can boldly believe and trust God for yourself, you must begin to do the same for others. You can have faith in God for anything whether it is a job for yourself, protection for your children or salvation for your friend. Faith is not just for you but for those who also need it. Just as my faith is currently working for you now, I am believing that by the time you finish reading this chapter your faith will be ignited and growing.

So, let's get you growing. If you are at a place in your faith where you notice you have been having issues believing God in certain areas, that should be your first target area. How about we put a little application to this faith factor? First, before we begin, I need you to do something for us. I need you to set aside your time restraints and preconceived expectations of how you think God should answer you. A lot of times, we stop our faith from working because we have placed God in a time box and an area of restricted movements. God does not have to bless you through the way you want Him to; He's

God, He can use anyone or anything. Please be open. Do not allow your impatience to cause you to stop you from believing God. Remember, a seed does not grow into a tree in one day. Some things must continuously be fed, watered, and fertilized in prayer by your faith. Have you ever seen a seed planted and not watered, fed, or fertilized that still grew? Every seed needs time to grow. Allow your faith to grow.

But they have not all obeyed the gospel. For Isaiah says, "Lord, who has believed our report?" So, then faith comes by hearing, and hearing by the word of God. Romans 10:16-17

Growing your Faith.

What our dear writer was trying to convey to us was an indicator of an answer. If every time we find ourselves struggling to believe, it may be because the report of the gospel has not been broadcasted. Your obedience to the gospel is a direct result of the measure of your faith because we believe based on our acceptance of the report. That report is the word of God. As we hear it, we see its truth, and as we see its truth, we are ignited in our faith. The more we hear with an ear to hear and receive what it is saying, the more we grow in our faith. Be careful not to give ear to things that do not promote the God-kind of faith. There are so many sounds fighting for the attention of your faith. Sounds such as those who speak against what God may want to do in your life of what you may be trying to believe God to do. Those unproductive sounds produce an unproductive faith. You we may not have considered it, but faith can be in anything. The moment you believe anything other than the word of God, that negative report in which you chose to believe became the object of your faith. For example, the word of God clearly says that you can do all things through Christ who strengthens you. Believing anything otherwise is a direct opposite of the word's report and is, therefore, proof of your faith being in the wrong place instead of in the word of God. But the good news is just as we rehearse skills, we rehearse the voice of faith, and as you hear, you grow…

So then faith comes by hearing, and hearing by the word of God. ^{Romans 10:17}

Our job then becomes positioning ourselves for growth. How? Well, we position ourselves in a few ways. Searching the word of God and writing down scriptures that relate to or enforce what you are attempting to grow in faith in. If you desired to be financially stable or get out of debt, you might decide to use the scripture that speaks about being a lender and not a borrower. It may take a little homework on your part, but the benefits will be rewarding. Standing on the word of God brings about the most promising results because God's word is forever true. It is already settled in heaven. It does not return without complete accomplishment of what it was spoken and declared to do because God is not a man, He cannot lie. All promises of God are yes and amen. Meaning they have been approved and are ready to be so unto you in your life.

Do the work.

The purpose for writing down scripture(s) is to have a clear picture of your vision for your faith. Writing your vision is what you desire to see through your faith because your prayer makes it plain for you. Making your vision plain eliminates confusion. Anytime your faith is challenged, you can go back to what is written to speak otherwise. Speaking would be another way because it allows you to hear that word that God has already spoken concerning your situation come from your own mouth. There may be times when you are alone, and no one else is around to speak the word of God into your life verbally. Sometimes your minister may not be available. The people or person you depend on for encouragement may be preoccupied or may need encouragement themselves. Thus, you have got to begin to speak to your own faith. When you speak to your faith, you cause it to grow even when it does not feel like it is growing, it is. Believe me, it is working for you. Speaking the word of God directly affects the state of our hearts. As our hearts are abundantly filled with faith, we then begin to find ourselves moving in faith. Our actions change, our thought process change, the stress is relieved, and our world begins to align with what we believe God for.

Earlier I emphasized using your own voice to speak that word of God that you are believing. I did not say that with the intentions of dismissing or implying that other voices of faith are not essential or vital. I aimed to prevent you from developing a dependency for something outwardly through another person when God wants you to allow Holy Spirit within you to speak through you to you as well. In Scripture, Paul, the writer of the book of Romans, asked the questions, "How then shall they call on Him in whom they have not believed? And how shall they believe in Him of whom they have not heard? And how shall they hear without a preacher?" We absolutely need preachers, sharers of the Gospel that speak the word of God when it is popular and when it is not, when it is hard and when it is easy, when it is accepted and when its rejected. If it were not for the men and women of God many would have no introduction to Christ thus there would be no reason to encourage you in your faith. God gave gifts as ministers, no matter their title (i.e., apostle, prophet, bishop, etc.) for your growth not for your dependency.

And He himself gave some to be apostles, some prophets, some evangelists, and some pastors and teachers, for the equipping of the saints for the work of ministry, for the edifying of the body of Christ, till we all come to the unity of the faith and of the knowledge of the Son of God, to a perfect man, to the measure of the stature of the fullness of Christ; that we should no longer be children, tossed to and from and carried about with every wind of doctrine, by the trickery of men, in the cunning craftiness of deceitful plotting, but, speaking the truth in love, may grow up in all things into Him who is the head-Christ. *Ephesians 4:11-15*

The purpose of the ministry gifts is to aid in the growth of your faith so that you-yourself can operate in the fullness of Christ. It brings the true women and men of God much joy to see those they have equipped, encouraged, taught, prayed with, and prayed for become fully grown and unmovable in their faith in God. Just as every loving mother or father wants to see their children become successful, the men and women of God desire the same for you.

Before you move on to the next chapter, I invite you to do a little homework first. Reading this book must be more than literature; there must be application if you genuinely desire effectiveness.

Take a particular need, concern, or request from God that has been difficult to receive an answer to. Find scripture(s) on that subject. Then study, research, and record what God says about it; make sure your request agrees with God's ways and principles. Some like to use prayer journals for this very reason, others use index cards, and some may even us technology. You decide, however, you must be able to access it easily. Write down your scripture and have it ready when you set aside time to pray. As you pray, quote the scripture as though you believe it is done. For example, "Lord, I thank you for your word that says...", "God I believe (say the scripture), and I thank you for performing your word in my life." The objective is to pray as though you already believe God has answered you. Along with praying scripture(s), find sermons, testimonies, and songs that encourage your focus area. Saturate your atmosphere with reinforcements to what you believe God for. Play those throughout the day to keep your faith engaged. This is an example of praying from the position of faith.

THE SECRET PLACE

But you, when you pray, go into your room, and when you have shut your door, pray to your Father who is in the secret place; and your Father who sees in secret will reward you openly. ^{Matthew 6:6}

I am sure by now you have heard the saying "prayer closet" or "prayer room". But if not, it is simply a physical place where those who are considered to have a prayer life dedicate a space in their homes to pray in. This can be very effective in developing a discipline to pray as well as creating an invitation for the spirit of prayer to be in your home through this act of symbolism. Not only does it promote dedication to prayer, but what better way to tell God

He has a place in your home. A prayer closet is absolutely a great thing if the space you create is used exclusively for God. It makes no sense to have a prayer place and not use it or to misuse it by mishandling its purpose and function. It would be as if you created a guest room for visitors, invited a visitor over but then parked your car in that very same guest room that you invited your guest into. I believe they would not feel so welcome. Would you? Thus, your secret place needs to be and remain sacred to you in how you use it. There is no need to say you have a sacred place of prayer in your home if it is not actually treated as though it is sacred.

Having a physical prayer room is not a requirement for prayer but is a tool used for prayer. Not having a prayer room does not make your prayer any less powerful than a person who has one. Your relationship and method(s) of communicating with God are between you and Him. It is a private matter that needs no comparison to others. Prayer rooms are sacred acts of faith and dedication of free will. They are used to facilitate intimacy with God in your home. The key is the intimacy, not the physical space, because when your secret place becomes intimate, regardless of where that is physically, God hears, and He answers openly. Your job is to make it intimate. You can very well turn any space into a secret place because the secret place comes from your focus within through your communication with the Father.

I am reminded of the moment in Scripture when Hezekiah put his face towards the wall to speak to

God. At that moment, he stepped into his secret place. Look at what happened to Hezekiah.

In those days Hezekiah was sick and near death. And Isaiah the prophet, the son of Amoz, went to him and said to him, "Thus says the Lord; 'set your house in order, for you shall die and not live.'" Then Hezekiah turned his face toward the wall, and prayed to the Lord, and said, "Remember now, O Lord, I pray, how I have walked before You in truth and with a loyal heart and have done what is good in Your sight." And Hezekiah wept bitterly. And the word of the Lord came to Isaiah, saying, "Go tell Hezekiah, 'Thus says the Lord, the God of David your father: "I have heard your prayer, I have seen your tears; surely I will add to your days fifteen years. I will deliver you and this city from the hand of king Assyria, and I will defend this city." And this is a sign to you from the Lord, that the Lord will do this thing which He has spoken: Isaiah 38:1-7

___

As you read, you saw that Hezekiah did not enter a separate physical location, but he turned himself to the wall to pray. At that very moment, the spot where he stood became his place of prayer. His turning is what we would relate to as the secret moment. We did not read that Hezekiah held a grand meeting so that everyone who was in the room heard him pray to God. Instead, he created a secret moment between only Him and God; that was his intimate moment. And God answered with an open favorable reply of adding fifteen years back to Hezekiah's life. This is proof that any death sentence can be adjusted if we would enter our secret place with humility. I believe that can be a physical death, just as with Hezekiah, a financial death, a relational death, or any other kind there is. The secret place can be your witness stand used to persuade the judge's decision of execution. The secret place is your game changer.

As we go back to the scripture of what Jesus said in Matthew some would arguably say when Jesus said, "go into your room and shut the door", that He gave us a requirement for a physical room. However, in my studies I found that Jesus gave those instructions to his disciples who were new to praying and were seeking to learn. If you were to read the previous verses of the same chapter in Matthew, you would find that the disciples were asking Jesus to teach them, meaning this was something new to learn.

Thus, as a basis, having a dedicated place to pray would be an asset for one who is just starting their prayer journey for quite a few reasons. One reason being a physical room to pray would help eliminate physical distractions during prayer, especially if you live in a home with others. It may also help others understand that a boundary has been established, and when you are spending time with God, that is your personal time that ought not be disturbed. Having a secret place in the home also helps to set a priority in the home. So, when Jesus gave the instruction to go into your room and shut the door, on a surface level, that could be precisely what He meant. But my suggestion to you is to go deeper in your interpretation to expand your revelation from the surface of a fixed place. Jesus was not mandating that the only place one should or could pray was to be shut up in a room. I believe another purpose for Him saying such was to give us a sense of prioritized intimacy that must be present, a sense of reverence when going into a mode of prayer. He was combating the formalities of the stigma of needing to be seen when praying.

And when you pray, you shall not be like the hypocrites. For they love to pray standing in the synagogues and on the corners of the streets, that they may be seen by men. Assuredly, I say to you, they have their reward.
Matthew 6:5

Jesus was unteaching his disciples by telling them not to engage prayer in the same way they had seen other men pray, which was before a crowd to be seen. This verse tells us exactly why those who pray to be seen never see answered prayers. Their answer to their prayer is to be seen, but when we want God to provide us with results, He answers by responding to the secret place.

Where is the secret place?

As we follow the ministry of Christ, we see that He often went up to the mountain to pray. I seriously doubt the mountain had a door and cannot quite imagine a mountain with a traditional room either, but it was His secret place. So, do not get caught up in the religiosity of creating a physical box to pray. Instead, embrace the idea of creating a limitless environment where prayer can happen at any moment intimately through your created secret place.

He who dwells in the secret place of the Most High Shall abide under the shadow of the Almighty. Psalm 91:1

When David penned these words, he gave us a sense of location as it relates to the secret place while admonishing us to dwell there. Dwell, meaning to be in a specific place. If we are going to dwell in the secret place, we must understand that it is a continually accessed place. For example, your home is your dwelling place, and at any given moment you are cleared for passage in and out of your home without legal restrictions; you are never trespassing whenever you choose to enter. Dwelling in the secret place parallels with your home. It is literally the place you go for safety, peace, replenishment, rearing, and preparation among other things, before going back out into the world. The amazing part about the secret place is abiding under the shadow of the Almighty. Naturally, when we think of a shadow, we often are in the mind of a dark image resulting from light being blocked. That is a correct thought. However, a shadow is also a trace of an object. Thus, if we are abiding under the shadow of the Almighty, we are living in the trace of God. The secret place provides us with a boundary that has been restricted to the imagery of God. That is why when you encounter those who live in the secret place, you can tell there is always a difference in them. Because they live in the trace, under the Shadow of God, as He moves, they move. Where is the secret place? His presence, my love, in His presence.

Fortunately for us, God's presence is not always like the presence of some people. His presence is where you receive your superpower, which is waiting for you in the secret place. Often, we tend to have a hard time entering His presence for many reasons, one being condemnation, but at that moment, we fail to realize that condemnation is not of God. Jesus did not come to condemn you but to save you. Thus, the presence of God is what I am happy to call a "judgement-free zone", a place to be authentically you. God already knows the real you. Do you know that you were created in a secret place, fashioned by Him?

For You formed my inward parts; You covered me in my mother's womb. I will praise You, for I am fearfully and wonderfully made; Marvelous are Your works, And that my soul knows very well. My frame was not hidden from You, When I was made in secret, And skillfully wrought in the lowest parts of the earth. Your eyes saw my substance, being yet unformed. And in Your book, they all were written, The days fashioned for me, When as yet there were none of them. How precious also are Your thoughts to me, O God! How great is the sum of them! Psalm 139:13-17

God knows you and the intent of your heart. He knows the number of hairs on your head, and every fiber of your being. There is no reason to be ashamed or insecure about going before Him. He is not afraid of your emotions or your flaws. You can be furious, you can be joyful, and you can also be hurting. He has all your proclivities covered, the good and bad. I believe we have adopted a wrong sense of theology in thinking that prayer is a gift of sorts to God from us as if we are doing God a favor or rewarding Him. Prayer is not for God but is a privilege provided to us, for us. For it is His love that has granted us the resource of prayer. However, if we choose not to use the resource, God will not cease from being God. We would be wise to take advantage of the opportunity to enter His presence as often as we can.

ENTER HIS GATES

Enter into His gates with thanksgiving, And into His courts with praise. Be thankful to Him and bless His name. Psalm 100:4

Many have made accessing the presence of God so difficult, and some have presented it to be a type of ritual of sorts. But, in truth, it is not hard at all to enter the presence of God. I believe the key to the gate opening refers us back to our state of the heart but from a bit of a different angle. Previously we talked about your changed heart being in a place of belief in God. Now that you believe in Him, movement into His presence requires another dimension of your heart being in alignment. This dimension of your heart deals with the state in which how you relate to God. As we look at the Scripture, it tells us that there is a place to be, which is in His gates. We can conclude that a gate is a passageway it separates one thing from another as it creates a boundary. Gates determine whether we are in or out. Just as there are gated communities that require access codes, I believe the scripture has given us two access codes as well. Think of it this way, we first drive to the gates, punch in the code, and then go further to turn off the alarm at the residence as we go further into the property's core. I really hope you are getting the picture I am trying to paint. Can you see it? We have pulled up to the kingdom to see God in His glory. Our first code when we arrive at the gate of the Prayer Estates is thanksgiving. I believe David, the writer of this Psalm, was trying to help us find our way. He made a distinction by giving us a specific directive. He could have said, "Enter into His gates with fear and into His courts trembling. Weep before the Lord, and repent with shame," but he did not. Giving a clear description of how we are to enter His gates and courts provided us with keys to the kingdom.

Thanksgiving is a form of worship. It has the potential to take the focal point off the receiver and onto the giver. When we are thankful for what God has done and most importantly who God is, it changes the mental narrative of our prayers. For example, ever have moments when you are angry and decide, "OK, maybe I should pray?" You start to begin to thank God for being God your unnecessary emotion of anger begins to subside as your mind recalls how great God is. You then begin to think about all the ways He has made, all the doors opened, all the times He has kept you, all the moments He has protected you. So, a Thank You springs forth even when feeling unworthy, because though unworthy, God still wants you to come closer and visit a while. As a father who anticipates the company of His children. Our thankfulness should be from a heart that understands the price paid for us to be able to boldly come before the throne of grace as joint heirs with Christ.

There is nothing like a heart that understands the value of its thank you. No one likes to continuously do things over and over for someone without ever hearing a thank you. We must never take the love and presence of God for granted. It must always be treated with value and reverence. I am pretty sure you can reflect on a moment in your life when before you received a hello there were requests, complaints, and grievances bombarding you without being celebrated for what you had already done. After a while, it probably drove you nuts. Can you imagine how God must feel when we forget how to come before Him, but instead immediately dump all our baggage of new requests before Him? Forgetting that you blew off the fact that you have already received a reason to be thankful for twenty-four more hours via the miracle of a new mercy that morning and still have an unused key while shouting from the other side of His gates. I believe this key helps us understand that without a heart posture of thanksgiving, no matter how loud we get, even with all the religious antics, we are still outside of His gates. You see, being thankful gives us access to wholeness, which is the corollary of prayer. There is power in simply being thankful. I am reminded of the ten lepers in the Bible in the book of Luke. Ten men were ill, and Jesus told them all to show themselves to the priest, meaning they were cleansed. All ten started to make their way to the priest, but one, noticing that he was healed turn around, fell on his face, and gave thanks to Jesus. Jesus noticing, saw that he was the only one of the ten to turn back to say thank you, rewarded him with wholeness. Something that those who did not say thank you, did not receive. Just to know that your "thank you" can birth your wholeness should spark a praise!

His Courts with Praise.

Praise, another key that has been provided us by David, this one now gives us access into His courts. So, now we are in, no longer outside the gates but now making our way further into God's presence. His courts. In my study over the years, I have noticed an interesting parallel between the spirit and the natural world. The way the things of God operated usually have a direct correlation to a natural element. It is almost as if all things created have a likeness of the genius of God of sorts. To me, it only makes sense to think that everything created by man has a mirror to a formula spiritually because we were created in the image and likeness of God, who is Spirit. So, in essence, all things created have an origin of an atom of His image and likeness through us. We are God's filters into the earth. As I was researching the ways of the kingdom of God, I see the analogue of that in the way in which we have established courts with a monarchy in our version of a kingdom. The interesting fact is every kingdom has a royal court(s).

So, when David said, "enter into His courts with praise" he let us know how to handle the royal place, and this royal place is grand because it has courts, with an **S** which means its plural. Anytime you enter a royal court of a Kingdom, you are entering a royal family household. Your praise gives you the key to the royal court! After you have thankfully entered the gate, release praise because you know that you are of the royal family of God. The household of God is in His courts and praise is the access code. The household of faith should have a whole new meaning now. Glory to God! We have shifted from outside of the gates with our "thank you God, for the privilege of coming before the throne through the price paid by Jesus Christ." Then to having been adopted into the beloved and are now blessing God because we know we are welcomed as the royal family into the household. Now let us pray.

THE MODEL PRAYER

Before we go any further, we must establish an understanding that this entire book is centered around the model prayer and is designed to help you grow in your prayer life. As you will read, I am in no way suggesting that you only stick to the model verbatim. Prayer is dimensional, and there are different types of prayer as well as other amazing books that have been written. However, in PRAYER101, we are starting at the foundation, the first recorded lesson given by Jesus. I intend to illuminate the message behind the model, to open the model for examination so that you can have a clear understanding of the way Jesus was teaching and why it was so effective. Just as in a biology lab, we are dissecting the model prayer to better understand its power and precision. There are many ways to use the model prayer as a guide; however, having the tools to use the model and translating it to today's vernacular will significantly benefit you.

And Jesus said,

⁹In this manner, therefore, pray: Our Father in heaven, Hallowed be Your name.

¹⁰Your kingdom come. Your will be done On earth as it is in heaven.

11Give us this day our daily bread.

¹²And forgive us our debts, as we forgive our debtors.

¹³And do not lead us into temptation, but deliver us from the evil one. For Yours is the kingdom and the power and the glory forever.

Amen.

Matthew 6:9-13

WHO ART IN HEAVEN

As we read Matthew 6:9-13, we find ourselves in the middle of a conversation between Jesus and his disciples, who had realized something was missing. They made an assessment based on what they saw as effective compared to what they had experienced as a ritualistic act of religion. I can imagine they collectively concluded that this dialogue might have been their missing link to accessing the same power they witnessed Christ operating in to do miracles. So, they asked Jesus, "teach us how to pray." In response to His disciples asking Him to teach them how to pray Jesus began, class was now in session. This is where we get the saying of "model prayer" because it was provided as a template.

When we think of models, we use them to provide an image or prototype of what a particular thing has the potential to be. For example, when purchasing a home in a new subdivision, the developer will provide a model home for those who are interested in joining the community but may need to see an idea of what that community would look like once built. Models also give us the ability to customize; however, no matter the customization, you will always find the model at the core. Just as in model homes, there are specific details that the developer chooses not to leave out because of their significance. I believe the same applies to the model prayer that Jesus, the developer, highlighted as well. The very fact that Jesus began this model with the word "OUR", says something of great significance to me that I believe has been given with the intention of teaching us.

OUR.

Our is a word that is used for inclusion. When someone says "our," they are speaking on behalf of themselves as well as others. Thus, Our Father would mean I am praying to God, who is the Father of those who are disciples (also known as believers). Jesus was teaching His disciples; He was not teaching those who were not His followers because they were not considered to be in the family. Remember, praying to a God whom you do not believe in is counterproductive. Why would Christ teach a nonbeliever to pray when faith is the factor to God moving on behalf of your prayer. When going before God, we go before Him acknowledging that He is Our Father. This also takes the selfish edge off prayer. That mindset that prayer is only about what we want and what we need individually and is not for the benefit of anyone else is entirely incorrect. As we go through the entire model, you will see that Christ used words like "our" and "us" more than once. Yes, we have personal things that we are concerned about and want to speak to God about, but prayer is more than that. It is an opportunity for you to speak to your Father for the benefit of others. A true heart of prayer is concerned about everyone's well-being. OUR Father.

Father.

The one who protects, shepherds, and provides for His children. When we refer to God as Father, we are saying God is the one who takes care of us. He is the one who protects, provides, and produces for us. He gives us our inheritance. Embracing God as Father comes with understanding what we talked about before, the sonship, knowing that when His children speak to Him, He listens. Proclaiming God as your Father also acknowledges Him to be your corrector.

Many times, we want the provisions of God but shy away from His protection and reject His correction.

When you pray, know that God is your Father, the Father of your brothers and sisters in Christ, and desires to Father those who have not yet accepted Christ. We have a responsibility to pray others, and in praying for each other we-in-turn, will be praying for ourselves as well. This aligns our heart with the heart of Christ, who selfishly gave of Himself for us and is our chief intercessor. Meaning He prays for us more than we pray for ourselves. He goes before the Father on our behalf and has sacrificed Himself so that we may have life and have it more abundantly.

Who art in heaven.

We now know we are approaching God as Our Father, correct? So, the next thing we need to know is where He is, to be able to approach Him. When we say, "who art in heaven," we are in essence saying we believe and understand that God sits in a supernatural place of glory. Heaven is pictured to be the throne of God that far exceeds the majesty of all other universes. The place of splendor, peace, love, community, infinite wealth, praise, and worship. Several other gods can be prayed to, but only one God, the Father, is in heaven. Who art in heaven distinguishes your God from the others. It parallels the moments in the bible where God was depicted as the God of Abraham, Isaac, and Jacob. They were giving a direct description of which god they were speaking of. The God who parted the sea, who gave barren women children, made burning bushes speak, and dry bones wet with living blood. There was no mistake as to who they were speaking of; therefore, we must be clear when praying. Our Father, who art in heaven.

HALLOWED BE THY NAME

Remember earlier when we spoke of entering His gates with thanksgiving and into His courts with praise? Well, hallowed is a reverence and honor for something. It means to make holy or to be consecrated. There is no greater respect than "hallowed be thy name." It is the ultimate form of acknowledging the name of God in all of who He is. The Father, Son, and Holy Spirit all as one. When we say, "hallowed be thy name," we are setting God as precedence above any other name, including our own. It is an automatic priority that establishes itself at that moment as you utter such words of reverence. And as we do, we are proclaiming that we are putting God first above all else. It is another dimension of praise and worship, almost as if the two become one.

What does that sound like?

In today's time, we would use words like, Glory to Your Name, Blessed be the Name of the Lord or other adjectives that express the utmost honor and reverence we have for God. Using words that separate God from the others making Him greater would be a hallowed expression. There is a scripture that says, "And I, if I am lifted up from the earth, will draw all people to Myself." We want people to be drawn to God through our prayer, which is why we must lift Him up from the sounds of our voices in the earth.

Worship through prayer.

One of the key elements to initiating a response from God is the element of worship in prayer. Taking a moment to be intentional about your pursuit of God through worship in prayer is like the old saying that our grandparents sometimes would use. "Give me my flowers while I can smell them." In other words, it means to appreciate who I am to you now in this moment. Love on me now.

Have you ever found yourself going about when a brief draft of a sweet fragrance grazed your nostrils? Our immediate response is to instinctively look to see where such an aroma came from. Well, when we adorn God with the sweet scents of our worship, we cause that same reaction. God searches for the worshipper.

> *But the hour is coming, and now is, when the true worshipers will worship the Father in spirit and truth; for the Father is seeking such to worship Him.* John 4:23

Break your Alabaster Box.

Seeking after God in prayer is wonderful and you absolutely should, but if you want God to seek after you, add the element of worship to your prayer, and that is exactly what He will do. There is a way to transition in prayer from you searching for answers to the answers finding you. And it is wrapped inside of your alabaster box. A woman in the bible named Mary epitomized the essence of "hallowed be thy name" amidst a crowd who were not fond of her actions because they lacked revelation of whose presence they had been graced to be in. But Mary knew precisely who sat before her as she knelt.

Then one of the Pharisees asked Him to eat with him. And He went to the Pharisee's house, and sat down to eat. And behold, a woman in the city who was a sinner, when she knew that Jesus sat at the table in the Pharisee's house, brought an alabaster flask of fragrant oil, and stood at His feet behind Him weeping; and she began to wash His feet with her tears, and wiped them with the hair of her head; and she kissed His feet and anointed them with the fragrant oil. Now when the Pharisee who had invited Him saw this, he spoke to himself, saying, "This Man, if He were a prophet, would know who and what manner of woman this is who is touching Him, for she is a sinner." And Jesus answered and said to him, "Simon, I have something to say to you." So, he said, "Teacher, say it." "There was a certain creditor who had two debtors. One owed five hundred denarii, and the other fifty. And when they had nothing with which to repay, he freely forgave them both. Tell Me, therefore, which of them will love him more?" Simon answered and said, "I suppose the one whom he forgave more." And He said to him, "You have rightly judged." Then He turned to the woman and said to Simon, "Do you see this woman? I entered your house; you gave Me no water for My feet, but she has washed My feet with her tears and wiped them with the hair of her head. You gave Me no kiss, but this woman has not ceased to kiss My feet since the time I came in. You did not anoint My head with oil, but this woman has anointed My feet with fragrant oil. Therefore, I say to you, her sins, *which are many, are forgiven, for she loved much. But to whom little is forgiven, the same loves little. Then He said to her, "Your sins are forgiven." And those who sat at the table with Him began to say to themselves, "Who is this who even forgives sins?" Then He said to the woman, "Your faith has saved you. Go in peace."* Luke 7:36-50

This woman's willingness to give reverence and honor to Christ despite being in a room full of men who ridiculed her for doing so gave her a blessing she did not ask for. Her faith in who she believed Jesus to be, led her to invite herself into hostile territory into the presence of the only Man worthy of the risk. Her faith did not just stop there, but it provoked her to worship as she bowed to wipe the tears with her hair and kissed His feet. Her worship released an anointing that could not be ignored. We saw the conversion of a sinner through worship; ALL her sins were forgiven. She did not ask for anything. She did not try to take anything, it caused a scene, but I believe she did not even intend to. She just merely worshiped. Her silent act of "hallowed be thy name" said it all.

We can stand to take note of this woman. Hallowed be thy name is not about you; it is all and only about who God is and who you believe Him to be.

THY KINGDOM COME

"Thy kingdom come, thy will be done" seems to be one of those phrases that we quickly and boastfully say when praying. I remember as a kid sitting in church as one of the deacons would pray. We knew that no matter who prayed that Sunday when they got to "thy kingdom come, thy will be done" that meant we were almost done with the agony of hearing them moan, holler, and repeat the same prayers they had been praying for years. I wondered if the reason he kept repeating his prayer every Sunday was because God did not answer the previous month. After a few years it led me to believe God was not answering at all nor listening; I sure wasn't anymore.

What does "thy kingdom come" really mean? What does it imply or what was Jesus trying to teach us in this stanza? Pondering what Christ meant by "thy kingdom come" has led to quite a bit of insight as far as the intention of Christ in His style of teaching. I believe that He was not speaking only of the ways and attributes of the Kingdom. He gave an analogy to bring us into the realization of what the Kingdom really is and what the Kingdom encompasses. Naturally, one would think of the lifestyle of the Kingdom of heaven coming into the earth as though the earth would be overtaken by the infiltration of a physical kingdom as if it were an alien invasion that does not involve the participation of earth. For those of us like myself who have seen movies of an invasion of a nation by beings from a different universe have probably interpreted the kingdom coming to the earth to be like a motion picture movie. The difference would be heaven would not come to kill us all and take over in a hostile way, but a similar visual concept of an invasion. I used to envision an experience more like my image of what heaven on earth would be; no crime, no sickness, no poverty, everyone getting along, beautiful days every day, just peaceful bliss. Almost as if the earth would go through a metamorphosis transforming into the Kingdom of Heaven, our streets would be made of gold, and angels would fly around everywhere. It would be so majestic. Clearly, I made my own motion picture in my head.

That leaves us with the question of did Jesus really mean thy kingdom come? He absolutely did, but the way in which the Kingdom comes is what I would like to offer a different approach to. Throughout Jesus' ministry, He repeatedly demonstrated the ways and attributes of the Kingdom; when He taught the multitudes, He taught the Kingdom. Everything that Christ did was about the Kingdom. He literally was "thy Kingdom come" in the flesh. After all, was not it proven that Christ was sent into the world not to condemn the world but so that the world through Him would be saved? His entire ministry was to leave us with the blueprints of the Kingdom. He brought the Kingdom here on earth. He did it through miracles, teaching, signs, and wonders. Through His sacrifice. Christ taught us how to bring the Kingdom into the earth by allowing the Father's will to be done through Him. The Father's will was done and completed through Christ by aligning Himself with what had been predestined in heaven. This is how it manifested on the earth. When Jesus accepted the will of God that was written in heaven for His life on earth, the will of the Kingdom came to earth through His life on earth. When we pray, "thy Kingdom come" we are literally saying we want the kingdom to show up in the earth through the will of God for our lives that has been written in heaven for our habitation period on earth. Thy Kingdom Come, comes through you!

Now when He was asked by the Pharisees when the kingdom of God would come, He answered them and said, "The kingdom of God does not come with observation; nor will they say, 'See here!' or 'See there!' For indeed, the kingdom of God is within you." Luke 17:20,21

There is so much to say about this scripture alone. Many would question why Christ would tell us the Kingdom comes through a Pharisee. Perhaps Christ gave us another lesson of how He sees us based on who we are destined to be versus our current state. Could it be that Christ answered based on the will of God for all, to accept salvation by believing in Jesus Christ, who is the way, truth, and life. Or perhaps Christ wanted to explain to the Pharisee that the Kingdom can come through him too while breaking down the religious mindset that he had as it related to the things of God. He was correcting false teachings that prevented him from experiencing the power of God. Another time in Scripture, the writer pens of the traditions of men making the power of God of no effect. What better way to teach than to give an illustrated example, including those you are teaching? The religious mindset of a Pharisee emphasized what they knew and what they did as an act of ritual rather than a relational experience with God, which is why they would sit in the temples and argue religion or compete in their acts by wanting to be seen praying. Jesus taught His disciples that the Kingdom is not a place to spectate but is who we are to be.

The kingdom is here, but it needs to come forth. The kingdom comes when you show up in prayer to rescue someone from the enemy or when you stand against the enemy in your life. The kingdom comes into situations with results and answers to your prayer. Just as Jesus showed up into the earth. You show up into the lives of others as the Kingdom. You are an establishment fortified by a belief system or a way of heaven. When you say, "thy Kingdom come," you are saying, "God, I want to show the world your kingdom through me!" That is the Father's will, thus God's will is being done when the Kingdom is present in the earth.

Thy Will be Done.

The will of God is His word; get to know it, it tells us all what God desires for His children. God inspired every word written in the word of God. Thus, you can trust it is what He desires for you. Some scriptures say things like:

If you then, being evil, know how to give good gifts to your children, how much more will your Father who is in heaven give good things to those who ask Him! ᴹᵃᵗᵗʰᵉʷ ⁷:¹¹

Beloved, I pray that you may prosper in all things and be in health, just as your soul prospers. ³ ᴶᵒʰⁿ ¹:²

Knowing that the will of God is always for your benefit because He loves you with an everlasting, unconditional love adds much joy to prayer. He settled His word concerning you in heaven before the world was framed. He provided a plan for your redemption which was executed to perfection by His son so that you would have access to what was predestined for your life in heaven here on earth. This is why we boldly, confidently, joyfully pray, "thy kingdom come, thy will be done, on earth, as it is in heaven." We want to be ALL of whom God has created us to be.

OUR DAILY BREAD

Please do not ever think that God is not concerned about the natural affairs of your life. I assure you He is.

Give us this day our daily bread. Matthew 6:11

Take a moment and think about what that possibly meant. Do you think Christ was only speaking of food? Because most of Jesus' teaching style involved parables, I am inclined to believe that this may have also been a moment of metaphoric teaching in a sense. We all need food daily and asking God for such rightfully makes sense.

God knows what we need. He told us to take no thought for these things. Did Jesus contradict God? Nope. Now hear me out here. Do you know of the story of the unnamed lady in the bible who was hungry for healing for her daughter of an unclean spirit? In Scripture, this encounter was written twice by two different authors. To prevent redundancy, we will only examine what Mark wrote, but the other account is found in Matthew 15.

For a woman, whose young daughter had an unclean spirit heard about Him, and she came and fell at His feet. The woman was a Greek, a Syro-Phoenician by birth, and she kept asking Him to cast the demon out of her daughter. But Jesus said to her, "Let the children be filled first, for it is not good to take the children's bread and throw it to the little dogs." And she answered and said to Him, "Yes, Lord, yet even the little dogs under the table eat from the children's crumbs." Then He said to her, "For this saying go your way; the demon has gone out of your daughter." And when she had come to her house, she found the demon gone out, and her daughter lying on the bed. ^{Mark 7:25-30}

I know while reading, you may have felt Jesus' words were rather harsh. However, please consider a few details. She was a Greek which meant by culture they did not believe in Christ and it was their custom to worship other gods. They named their god "the unknown god." Remember at the beginning of the book we talked about one of the primary truths of prayer: it was for the believer? This very response that Jesus gave this Syro-Phonecian woman proves it. As you see, Jesus had no intentions of answering her prayer. He did not consider her as one of His children. Praying to God and not believing in Him never works. The only reason Jesus answered her prayer was because of her response of humility and faith.

When dealing with this woman, did you notice Jesus uses yet another metaphor? And this metaphor is one of children's bread. In His dialogue with her, He tells her that it is not good to take the bread that belongs to the children. The interesting part is she was not asking Jesus for food, the kind that we get from grocery stores. She was asking for a different substance. And Jesus references the healing of her child from an unclean spirit as bread that belongs to His children. Quite interesting, isn't it? So, do you still believe "give us this day our daily bread" is still salads and hamburgers? No, my love, it is a daily portion of mercy released to us for deliverance from all evil trying to defile us. It is to be healed in our spirits, released from anguishes, torments, and bondages that have come upon us. It is not food for the body but a daily supply of nourishment for the soul.

Understand, daily; we need the bread of healing of the soul because there is a need for replenishment every day. Each day can drain us of the previous day's supply. I believe this is another reason why Christ used food for this analogy. Because food burns, we constantly need it to stay healthy and strong. The type of food we eat even regulates just how healthy and strong we are. When Jesus was teaching us that we need God to give us daily bread, He was telling us that we need to partake of God's nourishment daily. We need to visit the store of His word and receive the fruit of the spirit, wholeness, and holiness. It is so beautiful that we are all on the same playing field in this one. Jesus did not place a status requirement on daily bread. He did not say only those of us on a particular level or only those who are babies in Christ need daily bread. But the part I love most is He said, "give," "US." He included Himself! Throughout the entire prayer, Christ creates an "us" moment to let us know that we are all in this together. Glory to God! We all need daily bread.

LET IT GO

For if you forgive men their trespasses, your heavenly Father will also forgive you. But if you do not forgive men their trespasses, neither will your Father forgive your trespasses. Matthew 6:14,15

Sometimes, the hardest thing for us to do is Let It Go. There are times when we feel as though we have been hurt beyond repair and offended beyond recovery. Not to mention, if those who have committed the offense act as though nothing happened. It is almost as if it adds fuel to our rage. We neglect to take the time to find out if an individual knows of the hurt they have caused, but instead waddle in our emotions. Our minds develop an impeccable memory as it continues to recall the incidents, pushing our flesh further and further past the warning zone of strife and into unforgiveness because we have decided to dwell on it. Of course, this is precisely where the devil wants you to be because he knows if he can get you to harbor unforgiveness in your heart, it will hinder your prayers and your relationship with the Father.

You may not have thought of it this way, but the enemy wants you to be like him. Think about it, he and God had a loving relationship at one point until he committed an unthinkable offense, sin, that he refused to repent of. Therefore, he was kicked out of heaven, completely out of fellowship with the Father as an unforgiven being. One of his goals is to rob you of your opportunity for forgiveness, so he tries to get you to be unforgiving so that God does not forgive you. Because of this fact, Scripture tells us to both forgive and ask for forgiveness.

> *Therefore, if you bring your gift to the altar, and there remember that your brother has something against you, leave your gift there before the altar, and go your way. First be reconciled to your brother, and then come and offer your gift.* Matthew 5:23,24

Scripture even tells us to leave without offering a gift to the altar. I wonder if that gift could also be prayer as well as time or something of monetary value that would be brought to the altar. Understand, when we go to our brother/sister in Christ to ask for forgiveness, we are allowing the nature of God to live in us. Asking for forgiveness aids in preventing others from being trapped by unforgiveness because the enemy wants their prayers to be rejected too. And if they are harboring unforgiveness towards you, as a result, their offering and prayers will not be welcomed by God. What better way to express the love of God to one another, than by preventing the enemy from causing your brother/sister to be stifled in their relationship with the Father.

And forgive us our debts, As we forgive our debtors. Matthew 6:12

This may seem elementary, but to forgive means, to stop feeling angry or resentful towards, or to cancel a debt. A debt is something that is owed, and that something can be money, gratitude, an obligation, appreciation, or liability. Most times, when one of our debts has not been appropriately handled by another person, we will find the root of our offense. As we seek forgiveness for those whose debts we have mishandled, we are to extend that same forgiveness to those who have mishandled our debts. We are to stop feeling angry and resentful towards others and let go of their debt to us. Let go of the resentments due to the obligation, let go of the anger caused by their lack of appreciation they owe us; let go of the frustration from their refusal to accept their liability; and yes, even let go of the rage from all money they owe us and have not paid. Cancel those feelings so that God can cancel the offenses you have equally committed towards Him. Let it GO.

How do you know if you have offended someone without them telling you? If you have noticed they have suddenly put up a wall, that is your proof; there lies the ofFENSE.

JUST BELIEVE

We will quickly get back to our walk through the model, but I think right now is an excellent time to pause for a moment to express just how important your faith is to your prayer. Part three has been about the hindrances to prayer. It would be very remiss of me not to discuss how faith increases your prayer and why a lack of faith is so detrimental. Faith is everything. It is not only how we please God but is also how we move mountains. Faith ties it all together, it takes faith to speak, but to speak faith, your heart must be a heart of faith. When there is a famine of faith in your life, there will be a famine of answered prayers. Jesus rarely granted miracles in areas where faith was not present.

> *Now He did not do many mighty works there because of their unbelief.* _{Matthew 13:58}

Scripture tells us how a lack of faith displeases God. Praying a prayer that does not please God cannot work; it is counterproductive.

> *But without faith it is impossible to please Him, for he who comes to God must believe that He is, and that He is a rewarder of those who diligently seek Him.* _{Hebrews 11:6}

We want to please God in our lives and in what we say and believe in faith in our prayers. Your prayer and mouth should be in alignment with each other and the word of God. What you speak should never contradict your prayers. If you say you believe, then just believe.

If we are honest, we can admit that usually, the root of unbelief is fear. Fear can stifle us in so many ways. It is one of the top reasons that we use to justify our unbelief and doubt. The only thing is when operating in fear, admitting that fear is the reason why you have not stepped out in faith rarely happens until you are ready to believe. Fear holds us because it never likes being exposed. What I mean is when you are reaching for something in faith, if fear is present, it will feel as though it is pulling against you in the opposite direction of your faith. Faith always stretches out and fear always shrinks backwards as a defense mechanism. They each have distinctive sounds. Faith speaks hope and belief in the word of God independent of outside influences. Fear speaks doubt and unbelief based on past and present outside influences. An indicator of whether or not you are in faith or fear will always be revealed by what you say, it is your sound. What you do is just as important, but may I submit to you that if you cannot speak faith, you will not be able to do any acts of faith. If you can speak faith, you will grow to "do" faith. For now, just watch your mouth.

Do not allow what comes out of your mouth to cancel what God wants to do in your life through prayer. What you say can move mountains. Jesus gave this vital lesson of truth to His disciples. They were approached by a man seeking healing for his son, who was suffering from epilepsy, but the disciples could not heal him. Even though they were expected to be able to and were given the authority to do so by Jesus, they still experienced a moment of praying for something that did not happen.

> *Then the disciples came to Jesus privately and said, "Why could we not cast it out?" So, Jesus said to them, "Because of your unbelief; for assuredly, I say to you, if you have faith as a mustard seed, you will say to this mountain, 'Move from here to there,' and it will move; and nothing will be impossible for you. However, this kind does not go out except by prayer and fasting."* Matthew 17:19-21

As you see, though Jesus also mentioned fasting, their unbelief was the first problem. I believe He was saying if you had believed you would have accomplished the task even though this task takes a bit more than just belief. Because this is PRAYER101, getting into the fasting part will have to wait for the next series. But let me translate the first part for you to give us a clearer understanding of the guarantees of your faith. Your belief can move any mountain when it is as a mustard seed that grows massively. Earlier in Faith Factor, we learned about how faith is an asset to your prayer. Well, the lack of faith can be one of its most significant hindrances. If you have found yourself in a place of low faith, I encourage you to "get your faith up." Begin to take time to grow your faith, removing all doubt and unbelief. Reading the stories of great wonders and miracles that God has done for others is a very encouraging tool in boosting your faith and fighting your unbelief. Find scriptures on what you are believing God for, write them down, rehearse them regularly. It does not matter what others have done, what they have failed at, what you have failed at, nor what does not seem to be working or may have been impossible in the past. When you feed your faith, it can move the mountains of government, education, business, media, religion, arts and entertainment, and family. But your faith must be fed! The stronger it is, the greater the momentum of movement it will have on your mountains.

---

*For Isaiah says, "**Lord**, who has believed our report?" So, then faith comes by hearing, and* *hearing by the word of God. But I say, have they not heard? Yes indeed: "Their sound has gone out to all the earth, And their words to the ends of the world."* Romans 10:16b-18

Just do it.

Before we move on, consider what happened to the disciples who were out fishing after trying all night and catching nothing.

Simon Peter said to them, "I am going fishing." They said to him, "We are going with you also." They went out and immediately got into the boat, and that night they caught nothing. But when the morning had now come, Jesus stood on the shore; yet the disciples did not know that it was Jesus. Then Jesus said to them, "Children, have you any food?" They answered Him, "No." And He said to them, "Cast the net on the right side of the boat, and you will find some." So, they cast, and now they were not able to draw it in because of the multitude of fish. ^{John 21:3-6}

I am not trying to advertise, but one of our famous footwear companies here in America has what I think is one of the best slogans ever. Just do it. I do not believe they intend the slogan to be spiritual, but I believe it most definitely is. "Just do it," to me is a prime example of faith and what I have heard others call blind faith. In this instance, the disciples had a "just do it" type of faith. Jesus gave instructions, and though they had been out all night in the same water and had not caught anything. They still obeyed the order to cast their net to the right side. If I were preaching, I would say Jesus was only telling them they had been on the wrong side all night and simply needed to come over to the right side. And many times, we do the right things the wrong way and should consider doing the right things the right way if we want to be blessed with abundance. Or that He may have been testing their faith to see if they had conquered their unbelief. Nevertheless, the point is, when they were told to cast their net to the right side, all they had to do was "just do it". Because their response was to "just believe", they were blessed beyond their expectations.

Now to Him who is able to do exceedingly abundantly above all that we ask or think, according to the power that works in us, to Him be glory in the church by Christ Jesus to all generations, forever and ever. Amen. Ephesians 3:20,21

NO DEAD WEIGHT

Therefore we also, since we are surrounded by so great a cloud of witnesses, let us lay aside every weight, and the sin which so easily ensnares us, and let us run with endurance the race that is set before us, looking unto Jesus, the author and finisher of our faith, who for the joy that was set before Him endured the cross, despising the shame, and has sat down at the right hand of the throne of God. Hebrews 12:1,2

Our dear friend Apostle Paul wrote this letter of encouragement and instruction to let us know of the drawbacks of weight and sin. According to Paul weight and sin directly affect our Christian race. As a track coach prepares his long-distance runner for the meet, Paul admonishes us to drop every weight that slows us down and every sin that causes us to trip or stifle our endurance. Sin is taught as an evident stumbling block. There are very few times when we do not know when we are committing sin. We have thought about it, premeditated it, planned our execution, and may have developed a habit of impulsive sin. Holy Spirit even nudges us when we are getting too close. Throughout Scripture, we are warned of the consequences of sin and have access to stories of how sin directly sabotaged lives. Though sin almost always feels good, its long-term impacts are not. We tend to find ourselves being led by sin into situations that we did not intend to be in because of our inability to resist temptation. Our model prayer expresses a need to pray to our Father for assistance with our temptation.

And do not lead us into temptation, But deliver us from the evil one. Matthew 6:13

There must be a trust in God to be led by Him. Be confident in knowing that as God leads, He will not lead you into harm's way. Sometimes being led is hard. Especially in dark situations that force us to feel our way through trusting in God. To not be led into temptation is like saying, "do not bring me into situations that will cause me to want what is not good for me." As I pondered this very phrase for a moment, I must be honest; it really startled me. Would God lead us into temptation? Why would He do such a thing? Isn't that mean? Why would God set us up for failure? This four-word phrase really gave me the blues until I traced the steps of Jesus into the wilderness.

Then Jesus was led up by the Spirit into the wilderness to be tempted by the devil. And when He had fasted forty days and forty nights, afterward He was hungry. Now when the tempter came to Him, he said, "If You are the Son of God, command that these stones become bread." But He answered and said, "It is written, Man shall not live by bread alone, but by every word that proceeds from the mouth of God." Then the devil took Him up into the holy city, set Him on the pinnacle of the temple, and said to Him, "If You are the Son of God, throw Yourself down. For it is written: 'He shall give His angels charge over you, and "In their hands they shall bear you up, Lest you dash your foot against a stone." Jesus said to him, "It is written again, 'You shall not tempt the Lord your God." Again, the devil took Him up on an exceedingly high mountain, and showed Him all the kingdoms of the world and their glory. And he said to Him, "All these things I will give You if You will fall down and worship me." Then Jesus said to him, "Away with you, Satan! For it is written, You shall worship the Lord your God, and Him only you shall serve." Then the devil left Him, and behold, angels came and ministered to Him. ^(Matthew 4:1-11)

If Jesus was led to the wilderness to be tempted by the devil and told us to pray not to be led into temptation, I believe that is a pretty good idea. Just reading through the different temptations that Christ had to face gives us enough evidence as to why we, too, should pray not to be led into temptation. Do you think you would have passed all three tests? I think many of us would have failed the first one, especially after not having had anything to eat for forty days. We may have turned that stone into a steak before satan finished his offer.

The good news is that Jesus did not yield to temptation. Therefore, we also have the power to resist temptation as well. The enemy knew if he could get Jesus to yield to temptation, that would be Him yielding to his authority. That would then disqualify Jesus as being the all-powerful Son of God. One cannot have power over something that they cannot resist yielding to. What qualified Jesus as a greater power was His resistance to another power or authority, which was the tainted power that satan offered. Guess what?! Christ now lives in you and you have that same power over the enemy as well within. It is up to you to choose to resist the temptations of the enemy. Your authority in God strengthens as your resisting power strengthens. One who does not yield to temptation is always stronger than the one who offers the temptation. Only the weaker vessel yields. You are delivered from evil by your resistance to evil. After satan realized his tactics and enticements were not working against Jesus, he left him alone. Then angels arrived to minister to Him.

We do not want to be led into temptation, nor do we want to be overtaken by evil. Right? Praying "led us not into temptation" sounds imperative to me. Gratefully even when we do find ourselves led into tempting situations, grace is still made available.

No temptation has overtaken you except such as is common to man; but God is faithful, who will not allow you to be tempted beyond what you are able, but with the temptation will also make the way of escape, that you may be able to bear it. 1 Corinthians 10:13

God loves you so much that He does not tempt you beyond your ability but gives you an exit. A moment to choose right or wrong. It is up to you. Might I suggest "deliver us from evil" translates to being moved from the final destination of the residence of evil. When I think of a delivery driver delivering a package to a doorstep-that packing is in route to a stopping point, a final destination. The doorstep that it ends up on is a direct result of the ordered route.

There is a route to evil, and it is ordered by temptations to sin.

You may find yourself in temptation, but sin is totally a choice. The next time you find yourself in a sinful situation remember, sin is designed to hinder you. It hinders every aspect of your walk with God, your relationship, your prayer, your fellowship, and your power in God. The enemy desires to use your sin to get you off course to disqualify your Christian race by destroying your witness for God. Don't let him! Take your power back. Resist, and he will flee.

SOVEREIGNTY

Jesus finishes off the prayer with a declaration of the sovereignty of God. "Yours is the kingdom, the power, and the glory forever." As we take a deeper look into the kingdom, we see it as the epicenter of Jesus' ministry. He came to show us the mercy, grace, love, wisdom, and culture of the kingdom. There was never a moment when Jesus portrayed Himself as arrogant, nor did He ever inflict abuse on those who followed Him. Knowing who He was, knowing His purpose and mission, and being loyal to the assignment until completion is a lesson for us all. No matter how many miracles were performed, He never took credit for the power He possessed through God. And every time the crowd tried to give Him the glory, He always redirected the glory to His Father.

My dear friend, the privileges that prayer avails to you can never be seen or presented as a work of your own. The sovereignty of God must remain in its place in your life. When God answers, be sure to never steal His glory by thinking you answered your own prayer. No matter how well you grow to articulate and how quickly you see God answering you. Even when you start to see the dead raised, sick bodies healed, financial increases, and supernatural occurrences. Remember to say, "Yours is the kingdom, the power, and the glory forever." This is how you see results.

AND IT IS SO

And I will give you the keys of the kingdom of heaven, and whatever you bind on earth will be bound in heaven, and whatever you loose on earth will be loosed in heaven. Matthew 16:19

Because your heart is right, whatever your pray will be done. Because you have taken the time to search the Word of God to understand the will and intent of Your Father, you can now pray in confidence. You now know the will of God concerning you and have the faith to just believe in his promises. No longer are you hindered by unforgiveness, fear, and doubt. Worship God in all you do and as you invite the kingdom into your situation, receive your healing for all your "dis-eases". Even when you find yourself in an impossible situation, remember Matthew 19:26.

But Jesus looked at them and said to them, "With men this is impossible, but with God all things are possible." _{Matthew 19:26}

AMEN MEANS, SO BE IT. PRAY LIKE YOU BELIEVE IT.

Therefore I say to you, whatever things you ask when you pray, believe that you receive them, and you will have them. _{Mark 11:24}

TEACH ME HOW

Let us pray.

Lord God Our Father, with grateful hearts, we adore You for being the unmatched God that You are, the God of Love and Wisdom. We invite You into our situations and accept Your will for our lives. We believe Your Word that has already said we are blessed and not cursed, we are above only and not beneath. You have daily loaded us with benefits. Your desire for us is to prosper and be in health as our souls prosper. You told us to cast our cares upon You for You care for us. You said because we have learned to dwell in Your secret place, we shall live under the protection of Your shadow. Father, we believe Your Word that has already been settled in heaven. We say let Your Word be established in the earth! Thank You for giving us a daily portion of substance that provides healing and deliverance through Your Word. We forgive those who have wronged us and ask that You would forgive us as well. Keep us from all evil and lead us away from the traps of the enemy set to tempt us to sin against You. Continue to give us the strength to take the ways of escape that You provide for us in those moments. You are the sovereign God; You are the all-powerful one, and we give You all glory that belongs to You. In Jesus name, let it be so unto us. And it is so! Amen.

AFTERWORD

When I first started writing as a teenager, I intended to be a different type of writer. I wanted to write for magazines and tv shows, even dreamt of writing scripts for movies. Over the years, I have discovered God has a greater purpose for me regarding writing. Though I may still get to do those things one day, I will say that writing for Him has brought me much joy. I believe I have been blessed with the opportunity to be a blessing to you, and I am on a mission to do just that. I pray a part of the mission was fulfilled today, and PRAYER101 will continue to be a blessing to you and those around you as you share your journey. I encourage you to find someone whose life would benefit from an enhanced prayer life, and just as Jesus did, teach them to pray.

Thank you for taking the time to invest in your walk with God. May your investment in a stronger prayer life change your world. I look forward to hearing your testimonies of miracles in cities, nations, families, businesses, governmental changes, salvations, and personal victories through your prayers. Until next time for PRAYER2X. God Bless.

~ QuiNina J. Sinceno, *Author*

To order more copies:

quininaj.com

Other published works:

Life of JOY: The Key to Transformed Living

SELAH: Poetry that Speaks

Connect on social media:

@quininaj

E-mail:

quininaj@gmail.com

www.ingramcontent.com/pod-product-compliance
Lightning Source LLC
Chambersburg PA
CBHW051403290426
44108CB00015B/2130